I0436405

People, Places and Things

Mary Edner

authorHOUSE®

AuthorHouse™ LLC
1663 Liberty Drive
Bloomington, IN 47403
www.authorhouse.com
Phone: 1-800-839-8640

© 2014 Mary Edner. All rights reserved.

No part of this book may be reproduced, stored in a retrieval system, or transmitted by any means without the written permission of the author.

Published by AuthorHouse 04/14/2014

ISBN: 978-1-4969-0572-7 (sc)
ISBN: 978-1-4969-0573-4 (e)

Library of Congress Control Number: 2014907037

Any people depicted in stock imagery provided by Thinkstock are models, and such images are being used for illustrative purposes only. Certain stock imagery © Thinkstock.

This book is printed on acid-free paper.

Because of the dynamic nature of the Internet, any web addresses or links contained in this book may have changed since publication and may no longer be valid. The views expressed in this work are solely those of the author and do not necessarily reflect the views of the publisher, and the publisher hereby disclaims any responsibility for them.

1. I first became famous through a 1957 book . . .
2. . . . that has since been translated into dozens of languages, including Latin.
3. My home is on a mountain.
4. I owe my life to a well-known Dr.
5. My heart was once two sizes too small.
6. For a time, my only friend was my dog.
7. I made my TV debut in 1966 . . .
8. . . . and became an instant Christmas classic.
9. Jim Carrey played me in a 2000 movie.
10. I live just north of Whoville.
    Who am I?

1. I am a natural beauty.
2. I've been around for almost 12,500 years.
3. I'm half American, half Canadian . . .
4. . . . but I'm made up of three parts.
5. I'm open for viewing all day, every day.
6. Marilyn Monroe came to me to rendezvous with Joe DiMaggio.
7. Lois Lane fell for me in Superman 2.
8. I was the wedding location of Office-mates Jim and Pam.
9. To some, I'm a barrel of laughs.
10. I'm a favorite honeymoon spot.
    Where am I?

1. I was discovered 2,000 years ago . . .
2. . . . in the rainforests of the Americas.
3. I was used in ancient religious ceremonies.
4. Back then, I was a bitter beverage.
5. When I got to Europe, I became a sweet treat.
6. In the 1800s, an Englishman created a bar version of me.
7. Some versions of me are very high in antioxidants.
8. A river of me ran through Willy Wonka's factory.
9. Women crave me more than men . . .
10. . . . but everyone loves my Kisses!
    What am I?

1. I'm originally from Malaysia . . .
2. . . . and wasn't introduced to America until 1876.
3. Harry Belafonte sang about me in "Day-O."
4. I get sweeter with time.
5. I arrive in the store packaged by Mother Nature.
6. I am loaded with fiber and potassium.
7. I come in bunches, each layer of which is called a "hand."
8. Surprisingly my peel is edible!
9. Yellow is my signature color.
10. I am America's favorite fruit.
    What am I?

1. I am a famous American woman.
2. I hail from Georgia . . .
3. . . . but today I spend lots of time on my New Mexico ranch.
4. I was once married to a singer from Texas.
5. I've been named one of the "Most Intriguing" "Sexiest" and "Richest" women.
6. My favorite hobby is knitting.
7. I'm known for my million-dollar smile.
8. My niece Emma and brother Eric share my profession.
9. I've been called a pretty woman-and I once played one!
10. Most recently, you could see me in Eat Pray Love.
    Who am I?

1. I was introduced to the world in 1946.
2. I was designed by a French engineer . . .
3. . . . and named after some islands in the South Pacific.
4. I come in only two parts . . .
5. . . . but many different colors and patterns.
6. "Bond Girl" Ursula Andress credits me with making her a success.
7. You might see me on the cover of Sports Illustrated.
8. Princess Leia wore me.
9. According to a song, I'm itsy-bitsy and teenie-weenie.
10. I'm often found at the beach.
    What am I?

1. I'm a North American native.
2. I was present at the first Thanksgiving.
3. My varieties include Ben Lear, Howes, McFarlin, Searles and Stevens.
4. I'm almost 90% water . . .
5. . . . but so airy that I bounce and float!
6. Although tiny, I pack a big nutritional punch.
7. A popular 1990s band was named after me.
8. My juice adds the color to cosmopolitans.
9. You can buy me fresh, frozen, canned or dried.
10. I go great with turkey!
    What am I?

1. I arrived in 1982 . . .
2. . . . and was the first of my kind to be born in a hospital.
3. My parents used to call me Wombat.
4. I spent five years at boarding school.
5. My father is an organic gardener, among other things.
6. We are never allowed to fly in the same plane.
7. I am left-handed.
8. I've been called "the royal dreamboat."
9. My mother was the Princess of Wales.
10. I'll probably be King of England one day.
    Who am I?

1. I am a big city.
2. More than 12 million inhabit me.
3. I am located on an island.
4. I am home to a real palace.
5. I was the setting for a 2003 movie starring Scarlett Johansson.
6. I have my own Disneyland.
7. My name use to be Edo.
8. People come from all over to see my cherry blossoms.
9. I love sushi!
10. I am the capital city of Japan.
    Where am I?

1. I was created by Mother Nature . . .
2. . . . and in 1982, was made into a national monument.
3. I am named not for a saint, but for a British ambassador.
4. I am located in the Pacific Northwest.
5. I can turn daylight into darkness.
6. I slept for thousands of years.
7. In 1980, I woke up with a bang more powerful than an atomic bomb . . .
8. . . . and created an ash cloud that encircled the earth.
9. Native Americans call me Louwala Clough, or "smoking mountain."
10. I am a volcano.
    Where am I?

1. Surprisingly, there is no place on Earth where I have never ever been.
2. Today, there are places where you'll run into me almost every day.
3. . . . though you won't likely see me in, say, Tahiti.
4. People often stick their tongues out at me.
5. I've always got six sides . . .
6. . . . even so, I'm known for my uniqueness.
7. I can be shaped like a column, a plate or a star, among other things.
8. I am a type of crystal.
9. Winter is my favorite season.
10. It took a lot of me to make Frosty the Snowman!
    What am I?

1. I am 39 years old.
2. I'm about the size of San Francisco.
3. My closest relative lives in California . . .
4. . . . but I'm located in Florida.
5. My founder never visited me.
6. My highest point is the top of a mountain . . .
7. . . . and you can see Pluto when you visit me.
8. I have a castle, but I'm not ruled by a king or a queen.
9. I admit, I'm overrun by mice.
10. About 20 million people visit me every year.
11. I'm known as the "Happiest Place on Earth"!
    Where am I?

1. I originally hail from North America . . .
2. . . . but today I'm everywhere except Antarctica.
3. I can be small enough to fit in your hand . . .
4. . . . or big enough to fill the back of a pickup truck!
5. I'm fiber-rich and high in beta-carotene . . .
6. . . . plus my flowers and seeds are edible.
7. I played a big part in a Washington Irving story.
8. One fairy godmother transformed me into a carriage!
9. Linus thinks I'm great!
10. My signature color is orange.
    What am I?

1. I have a pyramid, but I'm not in Egypt.
2. I was founded more than 2,000 years ago.
3. My population peaked in 1921 at 2.9 million people; it's now closer to 2 million.
4. I am the home of the first public art museum.
5. My currency is the euro.
6. An estimated 50 million tourists visit me each year.
7. The final resting places of Sarah Bernhardt and rocker Jim Morrison are here.
8. I share my name with one of the Hilton sisters.
9. The Eiffel Tower is my most-famous landmark.
10. I'm the capital of France.
    Where am I?

1. I was born in New York City.
2. My middle name is Wagstaff.
3. I portrayed a murder in the final episode of Perry Mason.
4. I don't play an instrument and I'm not known for my singing voice . . .
5. . . . yet I was inducted into the Rock and Roll Hall of Fame in 1993.
6. I helped start dance crazes, such as the twist . . .
7. . . . and helped Paul Anka, Connie Francis and Little Richard become stars.
8. I survived a "payola" scandal.
9. I enjoy counting down to the New Year.
10. My nickname is "America's oldest living teenager."
    Who am I?

1. I'm a native of Cape Cod.
2. My middle name is Italian for "Sunday."
3. I'm a popular television personality.
4. In fact, my talk show won an Emmy in 2009.
5. I've written a string of best-selling books.
6. You can see my face on a monthly magazine . . .
7. . . . or daily on The Food Network . . .
8. I made a deal with Oprah in 2005.
9. I popularized the term EVOO-for extra virgin olive oil.
10. I'll help you make a meal in 30 minutes or less.
    Who am I?

1. Although early versions of me can be found all over . . .
2. . . . I'm really a 20th-century American innovation.
3. My popularity skyrocketed after World War 2 . . .
4. . . . when developers put a cover over me.
5. I'm a hangout for teens . . .
6. . . . although seniors love to speed-walk around me.
7. I'm featured in a 1995 movie with Shannon Doherty.
8. I'm usually home to some "big boxes."
9. I'm huge in Bloomington, Minnesota!
10. I help you shop 'till you drop!
    What am I?

1. I originated in China.
2. I've been around for thousands of years.
3. Some believe using me improves your memory . . .
4. . . . but some just find me hard to handle.
5. Mulan used me in the Disney-animated film.
6. Like shoes, I come in pairs.
7. Apiece of music with my name is popular with beginning pianists.
8. I am usually made of wood or plastic.
9. You see me in Chinese restaurants.
10. I am an eating utensil.
    What am I?

1. I can be male or female.
2. You can find me by lakes, rivers, pools and oceans.
3. I might whistle to get your attention.
4. I love a high SPF!
5. I sit head and shoulders above the crowd.
6. I'm not a spy, but I'm always watching.
7. Ronald Reagan had me on his resume.
8. Baywatch is my favorite show.
9. I know CPR and first aid.
10. My job is to keep people safe in the water.
    What am I?

1. Although I am a native of the Middle East . . .
2. I was a favorite of George Washington . . .
3. . . . and today I'm an official symbol of the U.S.
4. The British once fought a war in my name.
5. My hybrids have nothing to do with fuel economy.
6. Bette Midler and Nat King Cole had hits about me.
7. I am beautiful, but I can be quite prickly.
8. I'm often sold by the dozen.
9. I am a traditional symbol of love.
10. You'll see more of me on Valentine's Day than on any other day of the year!
    What am I?

1. I am an American original.
2. Winter is my favorite season.
3. I made my big debut in 1965.
4. Back then, I was called a "Snufer" . . .
5. . . . and it's been downhill ever since.
6. I tend to be more popular with youngsters than oldsters.
7. Sometimes I'm "regular," sometimes I'm "goofy."
8. I earned my first Olympic medals in 1998.
9. My most famous devotee is nicknamed the "Flying Tomato."
10. You can use me to descend a snowy mountain slope.
    What am I?

1. I'm a popular accessory.
2. In the U.S., more than 40 millions girls and boys consider me a must-have.
3. I have my own national awareness day; September 21, this year.
4. I carry my own weight!
5. You can see me around town, at airports or in the woods.
6. These days, I've often got wheels.
7. I'm a big back-to-school item.
8. I play an important role on Dora the Explorer.
9. In some parts of the world, I'm called a rucksack.
10. Kids use me to tote their books.
    What am I?

1. I was born in Connecticut.
2. Now, I live in the Southwest . . .
3. . . . but I have a special love for the Pacific Northwest.
4. According to Forbes, I'm powerful: to Time, I'm influential.
5. I went to Brigham Young University.
6. I'm a writer . . .
7. . . . whose career started with a dream.
8. I prefer Jane Austen to Anne Rice.
9. I broke J.K. Rowling's record.
10. My first book was made into a 2008 blockbuster movie.
    Who am I?

1. I am retro and cool.
2. I was invented in Italy . . .
3. . . . and became a huge fad in the early 70's.
4. John Travolta and Jessica Alba own one of me.
5. I'm puffy, but not bloated.
6. Today, I come in lots of shapes and materials, including denim and vinyl.
7. Originally, I was pear-shaped and made of leather.
8. You'll often spot me in dorm rooms.
9. Despite my name, I'm stuffed with plastic pellets.
10. I mold to the shape of your body.
    What am I?

1. I am an American original.
2. My name was inspired by the movie 2001: A Space Odyssey.
3. I'm only nine years old . . .
4. . . . but already 100 million of me have been sold!
5. I used to come in only one color: white.
6. My hometown is in California.
7. I have a wheel instead of a mouse.
8. The Sony Walkman is my ancestor.
9. I can carry a tune-in fact, many, many tunes!
10. I am a portable digital music player.
    What am I?

1. My name comes from a Native American word for "big water."
2. I am the only U.S. metropolitan area with two national parks.
3. My average daily winter temperature is 67 degrees.
4. I was the departure point of Amelia Earhart's final flight.
5. I'm home to the world's busiest cruise-ship port.
6. I love dolphins; sometimes, I love marlins.
7. I served as the setting for The Golden Girls . . .
8. . . . and I gave CSI its first spin-off.
9. Snowbirds flock to me in the winter.
10. I am Florida's second-largest city.
    Where am I?

1. Dutch immigrants brought me to America in the 1800s . . .
2. . . . when I was an olykoek.
3. A physic's major would describe me as toroidal.
4. A 22-foot-high version of me appears in Iron Man 2.
5. I can be old-fashioned, but I'm definitely not square!
6. I'm up to 25% fat.
7. I was made by hand until 1920, when the first machine was invented.
8. Renee Zellweger reportedly ate 20 of me a day before portraying Bridget Jones.
9. I'm Homer Simpson's favorite.
10. I keep Krispy Kreme in business.
    What am I?

1. The oldest still-surviving version of me dates to the second century AD.
2. I'm not a vitamin, but my name is Latin for daily allowance.
3. I am often kept under lock and key . . .
4. . . . although I am not usually worth much money.
5. I may hear lots of gossip . . .
6. . . . but I can keep a secret.
7. Britney Spears sang a "Dear" song about me.
8. A WWII teenager's version of me has been translated into 54 languages.
9. Bridget Jones kept one of me.
10. I am a place to record your daily thoughts.
    What am I?

1. I've been around since 1943.
2. I'm originally from Sweden . . .
3. . . . but today, I can be found in dozens of countries.
4. I attract big crowds.
5. Zooey Deschanel visited me in (500) Days of Summer.
6. My favorite food is meatballs.
7. This year, my catalog was produced in 17 languages for 28 countries.
8. My favorite colors are blue and yellow-just like the Swedish flag.
9. FY1: I take a D1Y approach.
10. I sell a lot of furniture.
    What am I?

1. I've been around for almost 6,000 years.
2. Jennifer Aniston and Raquel Wetch are devoted to me.
3. In my original language, my name means "union."
4. I have more than 16 million fans in America.
5. I am a form of exercise . . .
6. . . . and can be done on the Wii.
7. I can make you stronger and improve your posture.
8. Some say I reduce stress and ease back pain.
9. Julia Roberts strikes some of my poses in Eat Pray Love.
10. My name rhymes with "toga."
    What am I?

1. Everybody says I'm cool!
2. I'm no square, that's for sure.
3. Global warming is one of my top concerns.
4. Gene Autry sang about me in 1950.
5. In 1969, a special about me first aired on TV.
6. Michael Keaton played me in a 1998 film.
7. I come in all sizes . . .
8. . . . but my record is 11 stories high!
9. I'm not a work of art, but I am a sculpture.
10. I usually wear a hat and a scarf; my nose is traditionally a carrot.
    What am I?

1. I've been practiced for thousands of years . . .
2. . . . and around the world.
3. Today, I am mainly a hobby.
4. A lot of people regard me as a stress-reliever.
5. I used to be associated with grandmas.
6. Now, people like Julia Roberts and Cameron Diaz like me!
7. Some people take classes to learn me.
8. No joke: I will leave you in stitches!
9. I am responsible for a lot of scarves and baby blankets.
10. I am related to crocheting.
    What am I?

1. I have my own TV show.
2. A feature-length movie about me is in the works.
3. Everyone knows my first name, but not my last.
4. My motto is "We did it!"
5. My sidekick is a monkey, but I also depend a lot on my mouse.
6. I love visiting new places . . .
7. . . . and I love mi familla.
8. My purple backpack talks.
9. I am a Latina girl.
10. I am a cartoon character.
    Who am I?

1. I'm a movie star . . .
2. . . . but I'm not a real person.
3. I made my film debut in 1953.
4. My name has a familiar ring to it.
5. I'm a little flirt with a big jealous streak.
6. I help people defy gravity, although I'm not a scientist.
7. I'm not radioactive, but I glow in the dark.
8. I live in a far-away land.
9. I've been a Disney icon for years.
10. My friends call me Tink.
    Who am I?

1. I am depicted on the flags of two states.
2. If you dream about me, it is a good omen.
3. I come in 2,800 varieties . . .
4. . . . but I am usually tall and slender.
5. I've got bark, but no bite.
6. My oil is used to make soap.
7. My leaves make fans.
8. A famous California resort city shares part of my name.
9. My fruit contains "milk" and "meat."
10. I am the original home of the coconut.
    What am I?

1. I hit the limelight in 1960.
2. I only dress in animal print.
3. My red-headed wife is almost as famous as me.
4. I drove a fuel-efficient car before it was cool.
5. I am very animated.
6. My job is the pits . . .
7. . . . And I have a rocky relationship with my boss.
8. I belong to the Water Buffalo Lodge.
9. John Goodman played me in the movies.
10. Brontosaurus burgers are my favorite food.
    Who am I?

1. With less than one million residents, I rank 44th in population.
2. But square mile-wise, I am the fourth largest state.
3. Ted Turner owns thousands of my acres.
4. I'm a place where buffalo roam.
5. My capital is named for a woman.
6. My name is from the Spanish word for "mountain."
7. Daredevil Evel Knievel was born within my borders.
8. If you visit Yellowstone Park, you might visit me.
9. One of my nicknames is "Big Sky Country."
10. I'm also known as Hannah's last name.
    Where am I?

1. Creating me can be an art.
2. I sometimes shed.
3. If you rub me the wrong way, you might get burned.
4. You'll find me at the Oscars, dressed in red.
5. If you're in trouble, you might get called on me.
6. I tend to lie around a lot.
7. Turkey and Persia made me famous in the 16th century.
8. In the 1960s, I was pretty shaggy.
9. People walk all over me.
10. My samples come in squares.
    What am I?

1. I often hang around celebrities and rock stars.
2. I'm seen on beaches, as well as on ski slopes.
3. I made my first appearance in China.
4. My popularity soared after my 1929 Atlantic City debut.
5. One version of me helped WWII pilots.
6. A newer version is also an on-the-go music player.
7. Jackie O put me on the fashion map.
8. The Blues Brothers wore my Wayfarers.
9. Dermatologists say I help prevent wrinkles.
10. I protect your eyes from harmful rays.
    What am I?

1. I've been around for 2,000 years.
2. I am very balanced.
3. I follow a regular routine.
4. Lots of people flip over me . . .
5. But at times, I am judged harshly.
6. My horses don't run.
7. I have rings without jewels.
8. This month, I'll be on display in Beijing.
9. My athletes chalk up for success.
10. In 1976, 14-year-old Nadia Comaneci became the first person to score a perfect 10 in one of my events.
    What am I?

1. I'm an American success – but not an American original.
2. I speak English and Spanish.
3. I'm not known for my good looks.
4. People all over the world know my story.
5. I deal with the world of high fashion.
6. I work in Manhattan, but live in the boroughs.
7. The Suarezes are mi familla.
8. I owe a lot to Selma Hayek.
9. Vanessa Williams plays my nemesis, Wilhelmina.
10. I love America, Ferrera that is.
    Who am I?

1. Aztecs decorated statues of their gods with me.
2. There is a museum in my honor in Marion, OH.
3. The first colonists ate me with milk, like cereal.
4. I'm sold worldwide, but mostly grown in the USA.
5. I am named for a sound.
6. I have my own microwave control button.
7. People butter me up.
8. I come in a box, a bag or a bucket.
9. You could say I'm in the movie biz.
10. I'm one of American's most popular snack foods.
    What am I?

1. I am a fictional character.
2. I made my big-screen debut in 1977.
3. I've been told I'm a little spacey.
4. I have a sister who can be a royal pain.
5. And my dad is totally in the dark.
6. I'm usually dressed in white.
7. My weapon is dangerous, though surprisingly light.
8. Two of my friends have letters and numbers for names.
9. George Lucas created me.
10. Mark Hamill played me in the movies.
    Who am I?

1. I first appeared in public in 1915.
2. Then, I was mostly yellow.
3. Today, I am mostly red.
4. I'm found all over the world.
5. I work 24 hours a day.
6. I am made of metal.
7. Part of me is reflective.
8. I am octagon.
9. Typically, I hang out on street corners.
10. I bring traffic to a halt.
    What am I?

1. I am actually a fruit juice.
2. I've been around for more than 6,000 years.
3. I was first brought to North America by Christopher Columbus.
4. I usually come from Spain or Italy.
5. I'm good for your heart.
6. I don't mix well with water.
7. My color often determines my cost.
8. My first and last names start with the same letter.
9. Change one letter and I am Popeyes's girl.
10. I am a main component of a healthy Mediterranean diet.
    What am I?

1. I'm originally from England.
2. At first, I was a teaching tool.
3. Today, I am just for fun.
4. I once was made of wood . . .
5. Nowadays, I'm usually cardboard.
6. Little kids like less of me; big kids and grownups, more.
7. Sometimes, I'm two-faced; occasionally, I'm multidimensional.
8. I get my name from the tool once used to make me.
9. If you drop me, I'll go to pieces.
10. I can be quite puzzling.
    What am I?

1. I have both a very public and very private side.
2. I cost $102,000 in 1957.
3. I am now a National Historic Landmark.
4. Inside, I've got a waterfall, outside, a kidney-shaped pool.
5. I'm surrounded by a pink stone wall.
6. Although I have air conditioning, I'm filled with fans.
7. I share my name with a Paul Simon album.
8. After the White House, I'm the most recognizable U.S. residence.
9. I am not a castle, but I did have a king.
10. Lisa Marie grew up in me.
    Where am I?

1. A novel about me was published in 1818.
2. The first film version of my story premiered in 1931.
3. Surprisingly, the novel is not named after me . . .
4. . . . it is named after my creator.
5. People think I'm scary . . .
6. . . . but I just want to be loved.
7. I'm afraid of fire.
8. Boris Karloff played me in 1931; Peter Boyle in 1974.
9. I'm not Kermit, but it's not easy being green for me, either.
10. Kids dress up like me on Halloween.
    Who am I?

1. I was a favorite in biblical times.
2. The colonists brought me to America.
3. I am a member of the rose family.
4. I am high in fiber . . .
5. . . . although 25% of my volume is air.
6. I come in a variety of colors, like red and green.
7. Gwyneth likes my name.
8. I'm a nickname for New York City.
9. Sometimes people compare me to oranges.
10. I am the state fruit of West Virginia and Washington.
    What am I?

1. I arrived in America more than 300 years ago.
2. I am mentioned in the Bible.
3. Although I never get hugged, I sometimes get squeezed.
4. I come in many colors.
5. My bunch isn't related to the Brady's.
6. The average person eats eight pounds of me a year.
7. Technically, I am a berry.
8. You can always find me in Napa Valley.
9. My vine has been accused of spreading gossip.
10. I can be made into jelly, jam, juice or wine.
    What am I?

1. I was born in the U.S.A.
2. I am a taller-than-average woman . . .
3. . . . and I have a very distinctive voice.
4. During WWII, I worked undercover for the U.S. government.
5. I have published many books.
6. My TV show on PBS ran for more than 10 years.
7. Dan Aykroyd famously parodied me on Saturday Night Live.
8. I came before Martha or Rachael or Nigella.
9. I helped Americans master the art of French cooking.
10. Meryl Streep played me in a recent movie.
    Who am I?

1. I am an artist who was born in Wisconsin in 1887 . . .
2. . . . and lived to be 98.
3. I received the Presidential Medal of Freedom in 1977.
4. I share my first name with a southeastern state . . .
5. . . . but I spend much of my life in the Southwest.
6. My illustrated autobiography was a best seller.
7. Joan Allen played me in a Lifetime television movie.
8. My husband was pioneer photographer Alfred Stieglilz.
9. Although I painted landscapes, sunsets, rocks and shells . . .
10. My best-known subject is flowers.
    Who am I?

1. I was founded in 1886.
2. I am an American icon . . .
3. . . . but my name was inspired by a town in England.
4. My fastest-growing markets are China and Russia.
5. Reese Witherspoon is my global ambassador.
6. In 1998, I opened my first retail store in the Trump Tower.
7. I was first sold door to door.
8. People knew I was calling when they heard "Ding Dong."
9. Mary Kay is one of my competitors.
10. I am in the beauty business.
    What am I?

1. My climate is semi-tropical.
2. I was the 18th state to join the U.S.
3. I am the only state that is not divided into counties.
4. I am named after a king . . .
5. . . . and was once a crown colony.
6. The Mississippi River flows though me.
7. I am shaped like a boot.
8. Ellen DeGeneres and Harry Connick, Jr. hail from me.
9. My favorite cuisine is Cajun.
10. New Orleans is my most famous city.
    Where am I?

1. I'm all-American . . .
2. . . . even though five other flags have flown over me in my history.
3. My name comes from the Indian word for "friend."
4. I was the biggest of my kind until 1959.
5. I share my border with a foreign country.
6. My largest city is named for a famous Sam.
7. I'm the birthplace of two U.S. presidents.
8. My favorite flower is not the yellow rose, it's the bluebonnet.
9. One of my top products can be kind of crude.
10. I am home to the Alamo.
    Where am I?

1. I originated in Southeast Asia.
2. Christopher Columbus brought me to the New World.
3. I am neither animal nor mineral . . .
4. . . . but I can be a noun or an adjective.
5. I share my name with a California county.
6. You can find lots of me in Florida.
7. My blossom is a symbol of love.
8. I'm the same color as my name.
9. I'm very high in vitamin C.
10. Millions of people start their day with a glass of my juice.
    What am I?

1. I've been around for thousands of years.
2. Early versions of me were made of charcoal.
3. I'm not for washing dishes, but I do contain a detergent.
4. I'm sweet, but not a dessert.
5. My favorite flavor is mint.
6. Back in the day, I came in a jar.
7. Today, I'm sold in a tube.
8. I'm usually found in the bathroom.
9. Most versions of me contain calcium and fluoride.
10. I help stop cavities.
    What am I?

1. I am American.
2. In my youth, I was famous for my revolutionary ideas.
3. My image is very preppy.
4. Ben Affleck, Jay Leno and Uma Thurman grew up with me.
5. I know how to show you a whale of a time.
6. I'm a die-hard Yankee, but would never root for the team.
7. I'm divided into six different-sized parts.
8. I'm not a city, county, state or country . . .
9. . . . but I border with Canada.
10. My lobster, cranberries and maple syrup can't be beat.
    Where am I?

1. I was born in 1910 . . .
2. . . . in Skopje, Macedonia.
3. At that time, my name was Agnese Gonxhe Bojaxhiu.
4. At 18, I left Skopje for Dublin . . .
5. . . . where I trained to become a teacher.
6. I moved to India and taught geography.
7. Soon after, I took the name people now know me by.
8. I won the Nobel Peace Prize for my work with the poor of Calcutta.
9. A 1999 Gallup poll named me the "Most Admired Person."
10. Contrary to what my name suggests, I never had children.
    Who am I?

1. I have five letters in my name.
2. I inspire people to play practical jokes.
3. Poet T.S. Elliot called me cruel . . .
4. . . . but Elizabeth von Arnim thought I was Enchanted.
5. My favorite gem is a diamond . . .
6. . . . and my favorite flower is a daisy.
7. Aries and Taurus feel right at home with me.
8. I can be a girl's name.
9. I've got an important deadline on the 15th.
10. I last for 30 days.
    What am I?

1. I'm well known in cities the world over.
2. On a good day, lots of strangers wave at me.
3. I don't mind being whistled at.
4. Many times people telephone to request my services.
5. An Emmy-award-winning ABC sitcom was named after me.
6. Harry Chapin famously sang a song about me.
7. With me, there's no such thing as a free ride.
8. But my fee is "fare."
9. Traditionally, I'm yellow, but in London I am black and in Germany I am beige.
10. I'm a relative of the rickshaw and the gondola.
    What am I?

1. I've never seen snow.
2. I am the capital of my state.
3. I am home to Shangri-La . . .
4. . . . and to America's only royal palace.
5. The Amazing Race visited me.
6. I am the birthplace of Bette Midler.
7. I call the continental U.S. "the mainland."
8. I am on an island.
9. My natives are Polynesians.
10. My most famous beach is Waikiki.
    Where am I?

1. I was born in 1958.
2. My parents hail from Ireland.
3. When I was young I trained as a boxer.
4. I am an accomplished flutist . . .
5. . . . but I'm better known as a dancer and choreographer.
6. Lloyd's of London insured my legs for 40 million.
7. I set two Guinness World Records for tap dancing.
8. Since January 2009, I've hosted Superstars of Dance.
9. I like to call myself the "Lord of the Dance."
10. Riverdance made me famous.
    Who am I?

1. I am home to America's oldest bowling alley.
2. I am a river city and a lake city.
3. I am the largest metropolis in my state.
4. I am located in the Midwest.
5. I am the birthplace of the typewriter and Harley Davidson Motorcycles.
6. Spencer Tracy and Liberace hail from me . . .
7. . . . and Laverne and Shirley called me home.
8. For decades, I was America's beer capital.
9. In fact, Schlitz reportedly made me famous!
10. I don't start with a lock, but I end with a "kee."
    Where am I?

1. I am a native of France.
2. My name is linked with romance.
3. Kings, princes, and nobles were my first lovers.
4. I've appeared in movies alongside James Bond and Miss Piggy.
5. Parties are my scene.
6. I'm under so much pressure I easily explode.
7. My coloring varies from golden to pink.
8. I'm bubbly, but not perky.
9. I've blessed the hulls of countless ships.
10. I'm everyone's favorite drink on New Year's Eve!
    What am I?

1. I was born in 1946.
2. I've written three best sellers.
3. I'm also a successful restaurateur . . .
4. . . . and I have my own beer, Land Shark Lager.
5. But you probably know me best as a singer.
6. I have eight gold albums and nine platinum albums.
7. Nevertheless, I have a reputation as a beach bum!
8. I share my last name with a famous Warren.
9. My devoted fans are called Parrotheads.
10. I created Margaritaville.
    Who am I?

1. You might see me at the derby, but I'm not a horse.
2. I was invented in Europe almost 200 years ago.
3. An adept American added ball bearings to make me more user friendly.
4. I've got wheels, but I can't drive.
5. At one time, I had a key.
6. Back in the 1970s and 1980s, I loved disco music!
7. I come in pairs.
8. One version of me is known as quad; another as inline.
9. Some people play hockey on me.
10. You can use me in a rink.
    What am I?

1. Monet, Manet and Cezanne each painted me.
2. Summer is my favorite season.
3. My name originated in 18-century France.
4. A movie about me made Kim Novak a star.
5. I'm often a basket case.
6. You've probably sat at a table named after me.
7. I see more ants than uncles.
8. I am Yogi Bear's favorite way to dine.
9. My name has two syllables, and both rhyme.
10. Most people enjoy me in a park.
    What am I?

1. I am an American icon . . .
2. . . . and a Dame of the British Empire.
3. My middle name is Rosemond.
4. I have won two Oscars for Best Actress.
5. I made my film debut at 10.
6. Andy Warhol painted my portrait.
7. Sex and the City's Charlotte named her dog after me.
8. I famously love diamonds.
9. I have been married eight times.
10. My eyes are violet.
    Who am I?

1. I've been around for thousands of years.
2. I'm a native of the Americas.
3. Columbus brought me to Europe.
4. Today, I can be found everywhere but Antarctica.
5. Grocery stores offer about 4,000 products with my name on the label.
6. When I'm distilled I can be fuelish.
7. I am associated with bad jokes.
8. Some people butter me up.
9. I'm all ears.
10. Most people prefer me on the cob.
    What am I?

1. I'm British.
2. I was born during WWII German air raid.
3. I visited America for the first time in 1964.
4. My middle name was Winston-until I changed it.
5. My son and I share a birthday.
6. David Bowie gave me a co-writing credit on his song "Fame."
7. David Archuleta sang one of my songs on American Idol.
8. I am in the Rock-n-Roll Hall of Fame.
9. I was murdered in 1980.
10. I was one of the Fab Four.
    Who am I?

1. I've been around since 2002.
2. I am of British ancestry.
3. I've got a competitive nature.
4. I'm not a sporting event, but I have finals and semi-finals.
5. I've got judges, but no court.
6. I encourage people to vote.
7. I've seen eight seasons so far.
8. I'm the most-watched TV program.
9. I'm shown in more than 100 nations outside of the U.S.
10. I'm a singing competition.
    What am I?

1. I was born in 1955.
2. I'm a native of Arkansas.
3. As a kid, I dreamed of being a pro baseball player . . .
4. . . . but I ended up becoming a lawyer.
5. I served in the Mississippi House of Representatives . . .
6. . . . but I'm best-known as a writer.
7. Nineteen of my books have been bestsellers.
8. Eleven of my works have been made into movies.
9. Tom Cruise starred in the first one.
10. I'm known for writing legal thrillers.
    Who am I?

1. I originated in ancient Rome.
2. Back than, I featured lots of chariot races.
3. I first came to America in 1793.
4. I'm on the road a lot.
5. I love a parade.
6. Dr. Seuss wrote about a boy who ran one of me.
7. There are some high flyers in my organization.
8. Some of my employees get paid to clown around.
9. The French word for me is le cirque.
10. P.T. Barnum called me "The Greatest Show on Earth.."
    What am I?

1. I am British.
2. I am a fictional character based on a real person.
3. My real last name rhymes with "fiddle."
4. A book about me was published in 1865 . . .
5. . . . and a movie about me was released in 1951.
6. My story has been told in 125 languages.
7. I love tea parties.
8. I'm most often depicted wearing a pinafore.
9. I share my first name with the Brady's housekeeper.
10. My creator's pen name is Lewis Carroll.
    Who am I?

1. The earliest depiction of me dates to 3200 B.C.
2. I can travel up to 55 mph.
3. I'm a "green" way to get around.
4. For me, a red light means "go right."
5. The 5ᵗʰ Dimension sang a song about me.
6. I'm often made of wood, but I can be made of paper.
7. I've got a clew, but I'm not a detective.
8. I can sometimes be a dinghy.
9. My top prize is the America's Cup.
10. I go fastest with the wind at my back.
    What am I?

1. I'm not a snob, but I can be quite formal.
2. I come in different colors.
3. I can be a noun or a verb.
4. Back in the disco era, I got kind of wide.
5. But in the 80's, I thinned way down.
6. Sometimes I come with a bow.
7. A lot of people wear me to work.
8. I am descended from the cravat.
9. I can be paired with a suit.
10. I'm a popular gift on Father's Day.
    What am I?

1. I once starred on Seinfeld.
2. I am considered quintessentially American . . .
3. But I can be found in almost every country.
4. Sometimes I'm sweet, sometimes I'm not.
5. Sometimes I'm cold, sometimes I'm hot.
6. In the 1800s, I was popular at breakfast.
7. Usually, I'm round.
8. You don't want me in your face.
9. Add an O to the beginning of my name, and I'm on The Andy Griffith Show.
10. A Don McLean song about me was a number-one hit.
    What am I?

1. I am a famous American.
2. There is a statue of me in London's Parliament Square.
3. Gregory Peck portrayed me in a TV movie.
4. I had a beard but no moustache.
5. At 6'4", I was the tallest of my kind.
6. Among other things, an automobile and tunnel are named after me.
7. I frequently stored noted and letters in my hat.
8. I was born in a one-room cabin in Kentucky.
9. The nation celebrated my 200th birthday in 2010.
10. My face is on the $5 bill.
    Who am I?

1. I've been around for more than 100 years.
2. I was born in Pennsylvania.
3. I'm so popular, 80 million of me are made each day.
4. It takes 95 of me to equal one pound.
5. I am a registered trademark.
6. I come with a paper plume.
7. I look good in shiny silver . . .
8. . . . but I change my appearance for some holidays.
9. I pack a shade over 25 calories per piece in most versions.
10. I'm not really affectionate, despite my name.
    What am I?

1. You can find at least four million of me in the U.S.
2. I can be a male or female.
3. I have a license, but I don't necessarily drive.
4. I can be found in almost every village, city and town the world over.
5. I work in my room, but I don't sleep there.
6. A 70s sitcom about me starred John Travolta.
7. My skills are always in demand.
8. I like the letter "A."
9. Apples are rumored to be my favorite fruit.
10. I decided who makes the grade.
    What am I?

1. I am a famous American of Scottish ancestry.
2. I have a B.A. in speech therapy.
3. I'm one of the highest profile motorcyclists in the country.
4. Like Hamlet, I'm known for my monologue.
5. I like to make fun of people in the news.
6. Night owls know me best . . .
7. But that should change with my new primetime TV show.
8. I won an Emmy in 1995.
9. NBC is my network.
10. I'm known for my prominent chin.
    Who am I?

1. I am of German origin.
2. I came to America in the late 19th century.
3. I have gone into space with NASA astronauts.
4. My name has two words.
5. Mickey Mouse's first words were the plural of my name.
6. I'm popular at ball games.
7. I can be used to describe a skier or a surfer.
8. Even when new, I'm well seasoned.
9. In Germany, I'm the wurst.
10. I'm usually served on a bun with mustard.
    What am I?

1. I am located in the Southern Hemisphere.
2. I am a former British colony.
3. My currency is the shilling.
4. English is one of my official languages.
5. I was a filming location for a 1985 movie starring Meryl Streep.
6. My natural resources include gemstones and wildlife.
7. I have been called the "cradle of humanity."
8. I am famous for my long distance runners.
9. My capital is Nairobi.
10. I am the birthplace of President Obama's father.
    Where am I?

1. I'm a boastful boy with a beautiful smile.
2. I do not know my parents.
3. I've appeared on stage, in books-and in films, beginning with a Disney movie.
4. Statues of me stand in parks in England, Canada, the U.S. and Scotland.
5. Thoroughbred racehorses, collars-even peanut butter, have been named after me!
6. I love Darling children . . .
7. . . . and I'm hooked on pirates.
8. I can fly-with a little help.
9. I will never, ever grow up.
10. My initials are P.P.
    Who am I?

1. I originally came from the Middle Eastern desert . . .
2. . . . but today you can find me all over the world.
3. My favorite time of day is twilight.
4. I'm what you call an omnivore-I'll eat anything.
5. My name comes from a German word that means "to hoard."
6. My mother is caller a doe; my father is a buck . . .
7. . . . but as a baby, I'm called a puppy.
8. I like to stuff my face with food.
9. A plush Zhu Zhu version of me is one of the hottest toys around.
10. I'm a cute and cuddly rodent.
    What am I?

1. I am a top tourist destination.
2. My motto is "Justice for all" or Justitia Omnibus.
3. I am home to the only Leonardo da Vinci painting in North America . . .
4. . . . as well as to America's largest library.
5. My favorite flower is the American Beauty Rose . . .
6. . . . but in spring, I love cherry blossoms.
7. In 1939, a certain "Mr. Smith" visited me.
8. I am named after an American president.
9. My most famous house is white.
10. I am the nation's capital.
    Where am I?

1. The first one of me was created in France in 1783.
2. George Washington was on hand to see my North American debut.
3. I'm often very colorful . . .
4. . . . and I carry things in a basket.
5. I'm not afraid of heights.
6. You could call me a drifter.
7. Jules Verne wrote about me in 1873 . . .
8. . . . and the 5ᵗʰ Dimension sang about me in 1967.
9. I helped Curious George see the city.
10. Richard Branson flew across the Atlantic in one of me.
    What am I?

1. I'm very beautiful.
2. In fact, Gerald Ford spent the summer of 1936 with me.
3. My name comes from the Native American Minnetaree Indians.
4. I was the first of my kind in the world.
5. I'm larger than Rhode Island and Delaware combined.
6. I sit atop one of the biggest active volcanoes in the world.
7. Bears, bison, coyotes, moose and wolves take refuge in me.
8. Yogi Bear lived in me
9. I am home to Old Faithful.
10. I am a national park.
    Where am I?

1. The first of my kind appeared in England in 1683.
2. Today, I'm found in towns and cities around the world.
3. My name begins and ends with the same letter.
4. You could call me a real show-off.
5. You often pay to see me.
6. My biggest version is in Washington D.C.
7. I'm definitely into collecting.
8. I'm a popular field-trip destination.
9. My boss is called a curator.
10. Ben Stiller spent a Night at me in the movies.
    Where am I?

1. I am a fictional character . . .
2. . . . who always work nights.
3. I'm a favorite with little kids.
4. In America, I am usually depicted with wings.
5. In France, I'm a mouse known as "La bonne petite souris."
6. Either way, I commemorate a particular rite of passage.
7. Kristie Alley played me in a 1997 Disney movie . . .
8. . . . and Dwayne Johnson played me in a movie in 2010.
9. The Easter Bunny and Santa Claus are colleagues of mine.
10. I leave money under pillows.
    Who am I?

1. I made my first public appearance in 2009.
2. My story makes people laugh and cry.
3. I am loved by both children and adults.
4. I have a one-syllable name.
5. My hero is a septuagenarian.
6. I'm sometimes seen with special glasses.
7. My story is very uplifting!
8. I love balloons.
9. I was made by Pixar.
10. I won 2009 Oscar for Best Animated Feature.
    What am I?

1. I was born in Oklahoma in 1983.
2. I'm an entertainer.
3. I've won five Grammys . . .
4. . . . and I'm a member of the Grand Ole Opry.
5. I was voted "World's Sexiest Vegetarian."
6. Some people call my fans "Care Bears."
7. Simon, Randy and Paula are my idols.
8. I've got something in common with Kelly, Taylor and Jordan.
9. I've known a "cowboy casanova" or two.
10. I was the fourth American idol.
    Who am I?

1. I was popular in ancient Egypt.
2. I showed up on European tables in the 16th Century.
3. Today, you can find me at the boardwalk or the fair . . .
4. . . . or in your own kitchen.
5. Yellow is my signature color.
6. But I can also be pretty in pink!
7. When I come with a "stand," I'm a summer tradition . . .
8. . . . and a favorite with young entrepreneurs.
9. Despite my name, I'm more sweet than sour.
10. I'm made with sugar and water, and a third ingredient that gives me my name.
    What am I?

1. I'm a big city . . .
2. . . . and home to the largest Chinatown in North America.
3. Within my borders you can ski, golf and sail all on the same day.
4. I rank as one of the world's greenest cities.
5. In fact, I'm the birthplace of Greenpeace.
6. I'm sometimes called "Hollywood North."
7. If you've seen Twilight: New Moon, you've seen me.
8. Michael J. Fox and Bryan Adams hail from me.
9. Apolo Ohno went home with medals after visiting me.
10. I am the biggest city on Canada's west coast.
    Where am I?

1. I made my North American debut in the 1860's.
2. Back than I was exclusively in New England.
3. Now you can find me in every state.
4. I love the great outdoors.
5. I'm something to write home about.
6. I'm into arts and crafts.
7. In a popular movie and its remake, Hayley, and Lindsey visited me.
8. Funnyman Allen Sherman parodied me in a 1963 song.
9. More than 10 million U.S. children make use of me each year.
10. Summer is my favorite season.
    What am I?

1. I debuted in May 2009.
2. I've got a split personality: I'm part funny; part dramatic . . .
3. . . . and I like dancing almost as much as I like singing.
4. I'm set in an Ohio town . . .
5. . . . but I'm really produced in Hollywood.
6. I've won a Golden Globe.
7. My cover of "Don't Stop Believin'" went gold.
8. My Cheerios are not for breakfast.
9. You can catch me on Fox.
10. My fans are called Gleeks.
    What am I?

1. I was born in 1955.
2. I am American . . .
3. . . . but Queen Elizabeth 11 knighted me in 2005.
4. I've been called a geek, which I consider a compliment!
5. Although I am a college dropout . . .
6. . . . I became a billionaire at 31.
7. Today I am one of the richest people in the world.
8. I have been on the cover of Time magazine three times.
9. My wife Melinda and I give billions to charity.
10. I founded the world's most successful computer software company.
    Who am I?

1. I am originally from northern Europe.
2. Long ago, people sometimes feared me.
3. Today, I am quite beloved . . .
4. . . . but not as beloved as my boss.
5. I am not known for my stature.
6. I'm very busy every December.
7. J.R.R. Tolkien claimed that I lived in Rivendell.
8. According to the Brothers Grimm, I am a shoemaker.
9. According to the Keebler Company, I bake cookies.
10. Will Ferrell starred as me in a 2003 Christmas comedy.
    What am I?

1. I am an American original.
2. My birthplace was a garage in Menlo Park, California.
3. Today, you can find me all around the globe.
4. I'm better than a detective at finding things.
5. My name comes from a mathematical term . . .
6. . . . and although my name is a noun, people have turned it into a verb.
7. I "speak" almost 40 languages.
8. I change my logo for holidays and special occasions.
9. I am listed on the stock exchange as GOOG.
10. I am the world's most popular search engine.
    What am I?

1. I can be seen in ancient Egyptian hieroglyphics.
2. I hung out with Tom Sawyer.
3. Today, Amazon.com stocks Star Wars And Barbie versions of me.
4. I vary in length from about 24 inches to 20 feet long.
5. I'm in every episode of the Andy Griffith Show.
6. I play a central role in A River Runs Through It . . .
7. . . . but my reel has nothing to do with the movies.
8. I am popular on camping trips.
9. I can be made from a twig or from high-tech titanium.
10. You can use me to get your very own "catch of the day."
    What am I?

1. To the ancient Greeks, I was a love charm.
2. Back than, I was purple, red, white or yellow.
3. By the time I came to North America in the 1600s . . .
4. . . . I was a hybrid of red and yellow.
5. Most parents and teachers prefer me to a stick.
6. Parsley, celery and dill are my relatives.
7. I'm loaded with vitamin A.
8. Follow my name with "Top" and I'm a redhead.
9. Caution: Eat too many of me, and you might turn orange!
10. Bugs Bunny loves me.
    What am I?

1. I never catch colds!
2. If I like you, I'll pick you clean.
3. If you stare at me, I'll feel threatened.
4. A 1960s dance fad was named after me.
5. I can weigh anywhere from 3 oz. to 80 pounds.
6. I appear every 12 years in the Chinese calendar.
7. I hang out with my friends in troops.
8. The Marx brothers used my name in a movie title.
9. I really do like bananas!
10. I'm curious-just ask the man with the yellow hat!
    What am I?

1. I can be very loud.
2. But you can't see me.
3. Some people are scared of me.
4. I have a dangerous companion . . .
5. . . . who's a lot faster than I am.
6. I'm not in a gang, but I like to rumble.
7. When you hear me, you'd better take cover!
8. According to legend, angry gods made me.
9. But, in fact, I'm caused by the expansion and contraction of hot air.
10. I'm always preceded by lighting.
    What am I?

1. I was born in 1975.
2. I am an actress . . .
3. . . . and a singer.
4. I've been nominated for the Emmy, the Golden Globe and the Oscar.
5. I'm not American, but I do the accent very well.
6. I'm not a writer, but I am a Reader.
7. I've been paired onscreen with Leo, Jim, Johnny-oh, and Leo again.
8. GQ airbrushed photos of me without my consent in 2003.
9. I played Rose in a 1997 blockbuster.
10. In 2009, I took home the Best Actress Oscar.
    Who am I?

1. I am full of vitamins.
2. I am found in towns and cities across the globe.
3. I'm not a link, but I can be part of a chain.
4. I have checkers, but not chess.
5. My first self-service version opened in 1916.
6. Seventy years ago, I held about 900 items. Today I average more than 50,000.
7. In the 1960s, I was the site of a game show hosted by Bill Malone.
8. The average U.S. family spends more than $300 a month buying from me.
9. Mr. Hooper was one of my proprietors.
10. You probably pick up different magazines while visiting me.
    What am I?

1. Leonardo da Vinci designed the first one of me in the 1480s.
2. I use a rudder, but I'm not a boat.
3. I can have three wheels, but I'm not a tricycle.
4. I have a tail, but it doesn't wag.
5. Today, I can weigh 196 tons.
6. Yet I can go faster than the speed of sound.
7. A 1980 hit movie was named after me.
8. Say "Jefferson" before my name, and I'm a 60s band.
9. Charles Lindbergh made history in me.
10. The Wright brothers introduced me at Kitty Hawk.
    What am I?

1. The Algonquin Indians called me "sinzibukwud."
2. I'm not stupid, but sometimes I'm thick.
3. In fact, I tend to dribble.
4. People tap me when they want me.
5. I can look colorless or golden brown.
6. I am graded from A to B.
7. I share my first name with a tree.
8. My favorite house is a Log Cabin.
9. I pack 40 calories per tablespoon.
10. Pancakes and me: perfect together!
    What am I?

1. I am a living American male.
2. I hail from the Motor City . . .
3. . . . but I made my mark in Hollywood.
4. I share my middle name with a famous Henry.
5. My sister became Rocky's wife, and my nephew The Family Man.
6. I'm good at giving direction.
7. I have my own vineyard in Napa Valley, California.
8. I am well acquainted with Oscar.
9. My daughter has famously followed in my footsteps.
10. I am best known for The Godfather.
    Who am I?

1. I was born in Brooklyn in 1954.
2. Before I became famous, I sold light bulbs over the phone.
3. I made the cover of Time magazine in 1998.
4. One of my shirts hangs in the Smithsonian.
5. My Jessica is not a Simpson or an Alba.
6. I'm known for playing myself.
7. You can still see me in reruns.
8. I love to eat cold cereal.
9. My show about nothing ran for nine years.
10. I may be an A-list comedian, but I made a Bee Movie in 2007.
    Who am I?

1. You might call me the original Survivor . . .
2. . . . but I'm better known for being inept than physically fit.
3. I met my boss in the navy.
4. And saved his life when he fell overboard.
5. No one ever calls me by my first name.
6. I spend time by the sea . . .
7. . . . and hang out with millionaires and other characters
8. My minnow isn't a fish.
9. I have something in common with Maynard G. Krebs.
10. Bob Denver portrayed me on TV.
    Who am I?

1. I've been used to beautify, to heal and as currency.
2. You can read about me in the Bible and on the walls of pharaohs' tombs.
3. I was also featured in a Dr. Seuss book.
4. In the old days, I got my color from marigolds.
5. I'm trans-fat-free . . .
6. . . . but I'm full of cholesterol.
7. I often come in a four pack.
8. Vegan versions of me can be made from peanuts.
9. But mostly I'm made from cow's milk.
10. Sometimes people can't believe it's not me!
    What am I?

1. I'm an American original.
2. I've been made for more than 70 years.
3. My prototype was handcrafted out of wood . . .
4. . . . but now I'm metal.
5. My inventor made me "For every boy and every girl."
6. I roll on four wheels.
7. I can work hard, but I also like to coast.
8. My favorite color is red.
9. Despite my name, I cannot fly.
10. Kids use me to haul friends and toys.
    What am I?

1. I am home to more than 1.2 million people.
2. Barney the Purple Dinosaur hails from me.
3. Many people visit my museum dedicated to JFK.
4. I have more shopping centers per capita than any other major U.S. city.
5. I am located at three forks of the Trinity River.
6. A bronze herd of cattle grazes in my downtown.
7. Mary Kay Ash launched her cosmetics company here.
8. My football team has won five Super Bowls.
9. Surprisingly, I have no oil wells.
10. Drop a letter, and I'm salad backwards.
    Where am I?

1. I'm originally from England.
2. Today, New York City is my home.
3. The first book about me was published in 1926.
4. It has been translated into 29 languages.
5. My first name was originally Edward.
6. My last name makes children giggle.
7. Ernest H. Shepherd drew me.
8. Disney artists first animated me in 1966.
9. Honey is my favorite treat.
10. My best friend is Christopher Robin.
    Who am I?

1. I had a starring role in the 1991 film Backdraft.
2. Kids are my biggest fans.
3. Everyone stares when I go by.
4. I used to be steamed all the time . . .
5. Now I'm just under a lot of pressure.
6. People pump me, but not for information.
7. I love a parade.
8. My favorite color is red.
9. I prefer Dalmatians to all other dogs.
10. Long ago, I replaced the bucket brigade.
    What am I?

1. Millions of people know my address.
2. I'm seen around the globe every single day.
3. I encourage sharing.
4. Tons of people watch me, but I'm not a TV.
5. I was Time's "Person of the Year" in 2006.
6. I am less than five years old.
7. I've been banned in some places, like China and Iran.
8. I offer you a chance at worldwide fame.
9. I'm like a high-tech America's Funniest Home Videos.
10. Without "you," I'm nothing.
    What am I?

1. I've been around so long, I'm mention in the Bible.
2. I am the main ingredient in the world's oldest type of wine.
3. Although people love me, I never get spoiled.
4. I've long been used in health and beauty treatments.
5. I'm popular at tea time.
6. I don't mind being spread thin.
7. I'm good for you, but vegans don't like me.
8. I can be a term of endearment.
9. I'm made from flower nectar.
10. Winnie the Pooh is my biggest fan.
    What am I?

1. I'm a Washington native.
2. I celebrate my 16th anniversary in 2010.
3. My original name? Cadabra.
4. I love books and lots of other stuff, too.
5. I don't mind traffic-in fact, the more the better.
6. I definitely deliver.
7. In France, I come with .fr after my name.
8. I love Jeff Bezos.
9. I share my name with a famous river.
10. On the stock market, I'm known as AMZN.
    What am I?

1. I am an America classic . . .
2. . . . that hails from Rhode Island.
3. I made my Hollywood debut in 1995.
4. In 1986, I gave up my pipe for the American Cancer Society's Smokeout.
5. Originally, I was partly edible.
6. Today, I'm made of plastic.
7. I was the first toy to be advertised on TV.
8. More than a million of me sold for $.98 each year I first appeared.
9. Don Rickles is my voice in the Toy Story movies.
10. I share part of my name with a vegetable.
    Who am I?

1. I am an American innovation.
2. Lots of people think I'm pretty cool.
3. Some people even claim they're addicted to me.
4. I'm sensitive to touch.
5. I can't sing, but I can carry a tune.
6. At first, you had to wait in long lines for me.
7. I was Time magazine's Invention of the Year in 2007.
8. I love Jobs.
9. Only AT&T lets you use me in the U.S.
10. My name starts with an "i."
    What am I?

1. I am native to the Americas . . .
2. . . . but my name is derived from a Greek word.
3. The oldest of my kind have lived to be 300 years old . . .
4. . . . while the tallest have reached 60 feet.
5. There are more than 2,000 types of me.
6. Some of my varieties are beautiful bloomers . . .
7. . . . and other varieties bear edible fruit.
8. I am a plant that requires very little maintenance.
9. I like it h-o-t.
10. Careful-I can be quite pricky.
    What am I?

1. I am very broad.
2. I prefer facts to fiction.
3. I am popular with students.
4. Look closely and you're sure to find me interesting.
5. I am housed in homes and in libraries.
6. My name translates to "general knowledge" in ancient Greek.
7. I share my name with a fictional child detective.
8. People used to sell me door-to-door.
9. I usually come in sets and am arranged in alphabetical order.
10. The name of a popular online version of me begins with Wiki.
    What am I?

1. I'm known for my big imagination.
2. I've been around since 1963.
3. My original language is English . . .
4. . . . but today, you can find me in many languages.
5. My story has been made into an opera and a ballet . . .
6. . . . and, in 2009 into a live-action movie.
7. My main character looks like a wolf.
8. I am considered a children's classic . . .
9. . . . although my story is just 10 sentences long.
10. Maurice Sendak wrote me.
    What am I?

1. I am a fictional character.
2. My story originated in ninth-century China . . .
3. . . . but it was a 1950 movie that really made me famous.
4. I am known only by my first name.
5. My feet are famously tiny.
6. My sister's step all over me.
7. My glasswear is not intended for drinking.
8. Julie Andrews, Hillary Duff and Anne Hathaway have played versions of me.
9. My curfew is midnight.
10. In Disney World, you walk though my home to get to Fantasyland!
    Who am I?

1. I made my debut in 2007.
2. I am a great example of Yankee ingenuity.
3. I can free up a lot of storage space in your home . . .
4. . . . and in your suitcase when you're packing for vacation!
5. My relationship to Amazon has nothing to do with the forest . . .
6. . . . although I have the potential to save a lot of trees.
7. People love my portability.
8. Barnes & Noble created the nook to compete with me.
9. Librarians and booksellers may not love me, but I love books . . .
10. . . . or rather, I love electronic eBooks!
    What am I?

1. I am a very popular book.
2. I am based on a true story.
3. I was at the top of the New York Times bestseller list for 57 weeks.
4. My tale starts and ends in New York . . .
5. . . . but in the middle, it travels around the world.
6. Oprah loved me!
7. In 2010, my story was made into a movie starring Julia Roberts.
8. My title has three verbs.
9. I begin with divorce and end with love.
10. I was written by Elizabeth Gilbert.
    What am I?

1. I originated in Sweden . . .
2. . . . but my name is Italian
3. . . . and usually spoken to express surprise.
4. I hit the airwaves in 1975.
5. People say I'm "catchy."
6. I inspired a musical that debuted in London in 1999 . . .
7. . . . where they added an exclamation point to my name!
8. I have something in common with "Bohemian Rhapsody" by Queen.
9. I helped Meryl Streep show off her vocal talents in a 2008 movie.
10. I was written and originally performed by the singing group ABBA.
    What am I?

1. I was discovered in China more than 5,000 years ago.
2. Today, I can be found in 80% of American households.
3. I come in different colors and flavors.
4. I should be stored in airtight containers
5. In Latin, my name is camellia sinensis.
6. I'm usually in hot water . . .
7. . . . but I can be iced, too.
8. Alice famously drank me in Wonderland.
9. The British prefer me with milk and sugar.
10. I sound like a single letter.
    What am I?

1. People love to dress up for me.
2. Queen Elizabeth, Babe Ruth and Courtney Cox have all seen me.
3. I only last a few minutes . . .
4. But my participants lose 15 to 25 pounds in that time!
5. You can watch me on TV once a year.
6. I'm not a pre-school, but I only accept three-year-olds.
7. I'm a Bluegrass State tradition.
8. I love a good mint julep.
9. I'm sometimes called the "Run for the Roses."
10. I am the first jewel in the Triple Crown.
    What am I?

1. I'm an American classic.
2. My name was taken from a poem by Ernest Dowson.
3. You may know me as a book or a movie.
4. My 1,037-page hardcover version cost $3 when it was published in 1936.
5. My main character is quite colorful.
6. A musical based on me is to open in London in 2009.
7. I am all about the 19th century South.
8. David O. Selznick produced my movie.
9. Vivien Leigh won an Oscar for acting in me.
10. Margaret Mitchell is my author.
    What am I?

1. I was born in 1958.
2. Jobs I've had include legal secretary, house painter and oyster shucker.
3. My mother wrote a book about me.
4. I live in Beverly Hills.
5. I've hosted the Oscars . . .
6. . . . and the Grammys.
7. I love blue sneakers.
8. In 2009, I became a Cover Girl.
9. I've got my own talk show.
10. I was the voice of Dory in Finding Nemo.
    Who am I?

1. I'm an American original.
2. I am not ecology-minded, but I do like green houses.
3. Get involved with me and you might go to jail.
4. Now Ridley Scott is working on a movie based on me.
5. Most of the time, you'll find me on a table.
6. A game show named after me aired on ABC in 1990.
7. I once lasted for 1,680 hours.
8. An estimated 500 million people have played me.
9. Many of my 40 squares are named after streets in Atlantic City.
10. I am a classic board game.
    What am I?

1. I was around during the Stone Age . . .
2. . . . and you can read about me in the Bible.
3. I come in many shapes and sizes.
4. I can be light or dark, sweet or sour.
5. My name is slang for money.
6. The poet Omar Khayyam liked me with wine.
7. Hansel and Gretel would be lost without me.
8. I admit it: I can be crumby.
9. A popular 70s band was named after me.
10. I am sometimes called the staff of life.
    What am I?

1. I was invented by the ancient Greeks.
2. Today, I am a regularly scheduled event . . .
3. . . . that millions of people participate in.
4. People who study me are called psephologists.
5. A day is named for me . . .
6. . . . so was a movie starring Reese Witherspoon.
7. I can make local or national news.
8. Washington was the first president to benefit from me.
9. I am a cornerstone of democracy.
10. I help people select leaders.
    What am I?

1. I arrived on the American scene in the 1800s.
2. Originally, I was used outdoors; now, I stay inside.
3. I come in many colors, but only one shape.
4. My weight varies, but not my size.
5. I was originally made of wood . . .
6. . . . but today I'm frequently made of polyester.
7. Homer bought one of me for Marge.
8. I'm often on pins, but never on needles.
9. You might see me in the alley, the lane or the gutter.
10. For me, strikes are a good thing!
    What am I?

1. I am home to four million people . . .
2. . . . and 60 million sheep.
3. My currency is based on the dollar, but my flag has just four stars.
4. I was the first country to allow women to vote.
5. I'm warmer to the north and colder to the south.
6. My kiwis are not necessarily fruit.
7. My Alps are larger than the French, Austrian and Swiss ones combined.
8. Auckland is my biggest city.
9. I am the setting for the Lord of the Rings trilogy.
10. My closest neighbor is Australia.
    Where am I?

1. I originated in New York City.
2. I've been around since September 2001.
3. I'm not a mystery, but I have clues.
4. I prefer reality to fantasy.
5. I require teamwork.
6. I'm not in NASCAR, but I do have pit stops.
7. I just started my 14th season in 2009.
8. I've won 11 Emmys.
9. Phil's my main man.
10. I'll help you see the world, right from home.
    What am I?

1. I am an American legend . . .
2. . . . even though I'm only 33 years old.
3. According to my mom, red is my "power color."
4. My name is Eldrick, but no one calls me that.
5. I left college after two years to turn professional.
6. Gatorade named a sports drink after me.
7. I was the highest-paid pro athlete in 2008.
8. My ex wife is a former model and we have two children.
9. My favorite movie is Caddyshack.
10. I'm the youngest golfer to win a career Grand Slam.
    Who am I?

1. I have 20 distinct layers.
2. Many gasp at the beauty of my colors.
3. I am the biggest of my kind in the world.
4. A river runs though me.
5. I was once a vacation destination for the Brady Bunch.
6. Kevin Kline and Danny Glover were in a movie named for me.
7. I am in a national park.
8. I am one of the Seven Wonders of the Natural World.
9. You can ride a mule down me.
10. President Roosevelt encouraged every American to visit me in Arizona.
    Where am I?

1. I love bright colors!
2. I'm not a flower, but I need rain and sunshine.
3. My true shape is a circle.
4. My bands do not make music.
5. My bow doesn't get tied.
6. I've inspired many poets, including Wordsworth and Keats.
7. L. Frank Baum's heroine wanted to fly over me.
8. Kermit had a connection with me.
9. Add Brite to me and I am a 1980s cartoon.
10. Leprechauns use me as a hiding spot.
    What am I?

1. I'm the largest and heaviest of my kind.
2. I hail from Africa . . .
3. . . . but you can find me on ranches in the U.S.
4. My eyes are almost two inches wide.
5. I can grow to be eight feet tall.
6. I can run up to 40 m.p.h.
7. My meat is said to be a healthier alternative to beef.
8. One of my eggs weighs as much as two dozen chicken eggs!
9. I am a bird, but I can't fly.
10. It's a myth that I bury my head in the sand!
    What am I?

1. I am another one of Leonardo da Vinci's bright ideas!
2. But the idea didn't become a reality until 1887.
3. Early versions of me were made of glass.
4. Today, I'm made of high-tech plastic.
5. You should wash your hands before touching me.
6. I almost always come in pairs.
7. I often come out at night.
8. I can be clear or tinted.
9. I am sometimes disposable.
10. I'm good for people who don't like eyeglasses.
    What am I?

1. I originated in China.
2. I arrived in America in 1857.
3. I am used for cleaning.
4. In a survey, people picked me as the number-one thing they can't live without.
5. I come in many sizes and colors . . .
6. . . . but only one shape: long and skinny.
7. In families, you'll find more than one of me.
8. Most people use me at least twice a day.
9. You put paste on me.
10. Your dentist might give me to you.
    What am I?

1. I've been around since 1937.
2. I'm credited with saving many lives during WWII.
3. There is a museum devoted to me in Minnesota.
4. I'm featured in a Tony Award-winning musical.
5. Find one version of me in grocery stores . . .
6. . . . another version in your computer.
7. I'm one of the original convenience foods.
8. I'm sometimes called "Hawaiian Steak."
9. Rearrange my letters and I spell maps.
10. I come in a can.
   What am I?

1. My water is more than 80 degrees Fahrenheit.
2. I am home to around 200 species of orchids.
3. My coat of arms features a crocodile.
4. I am located in the Caribbean Sea.
5. Columbus discovered me.
6. The coffee liqueur Tia Maria comes from me.
7. My jerks aren't rude.
8. Stella got her groove back while visiting me.
9. My Olympic athletes were portrayed in the movie Cool Running.
10. The Marley family made my music famous.
   Where am I?

1. I first appeared in public in 1935.
2. I've had roles in movies and on television.
3. I even had my own TV show, which ran on Saturdays from 1964 to 1967.
4. My first and last names start with the same letter.
5. I'm rarely seen without a red bowtie.
6. My girlfriend's name is Petunia.
7. I have four legs, but I walk on two.
8. I'm not a musician, but I like Looney Tunes.
9. I am on TV Guide's Top 50 Cartoon Characters list.
10. My goodbye is "Th-th-th-that's all, folks!"
   Who am I?

1. I was founded in 2004.
2. My name originally began with "The."
3. I hail from Cambridge Massachusetts . . .
4. . . . but today you can find me on every continent.
5. I have more than 150 million friends.
6. I'm not made of paper, but I've got lots of pages.
7. I am accessible round-the-clock.
8. I'm known for being very social.
9. I am a special kind of website.
10. I help you reunite with old friends.
    What am I?

1. I am from Japan.
2. I celebrated my 30th birthday in 2010.
3. I am a major icon of the 80s . . .
4. . . . which is why I'm on display in the Smithsonian.
5. My complexion is yellow.
6. According to a 1982 hit song, a lot of people caught my "Fever."
7. An animated TV series about me aired on ABC from 1982 to 1984.
8. Blinky, Pinky, Inky and Clyde are my enemies.
9. I was designed to look like a pizza with a missing slice.
10. I am the most recognizable video game character of all time.
    What am I?

1. I travel a lot.
2. To me, pointing isn't rude.
3. I have many degrees, but I've never been to college.
4. If I'm spinning, you're in trouble.
5. The earth guides me.
6. I'm magnetic.
7. Sailors can't get along without me.
8. You'll find a high-tech version of me in a GPS.
9. If you're lost, I can help you find your way.
10. According to a 2007 movie, I'm Golden.
    What am I?

1. My ancestors were first seen in England in the 1800s.
2. I made my U.S. premiere in 1913 . . .
3. . . . but I became a craze in 1924, when a collection of me appeared in book form.
4. Once, mostly children liked me.
5. Today, adults are my biggest audience.
6. I'm known for being shapely.
7. My favorite colors are black and white.
8. I was used in World War II to pass secret codes to the military.
9. You can find me every day in most newspapers.
10. The board game Scrabble is based on me.
    What am I?

1. Summer is my time of year.
2. You can find me in many American cities.
3. The oldest one of me is 99 . . .
4. . . . and is located in Birmingham, Alabama.
5. I love diamonds.
6. You can see me on TV.
7. Or you can buy a ticket and see me in person.
8. Visit me and you will hear the national anthem . . .
9. . . . and a song about peanuts and Cracker Jack.
10. America's favorite summer sport is played in me.
    What am I?

1. Most people call me by my initials.
2. I have a starring role on CSI.
3. My main job is giving instructions.
4. I am sensitive to X-rays and sunlight.
5. I can make blueprints, but I'm not an architect.
6. You are unique because of me.
7. I'm like a fingerprint, only better.
8. Crick and Watson revealed my double-helix shape to the world in 1953.
9. Many refer to me as life's building block.
10. My real name is deoxyribonucleic acid.
    What am I?

1. In my genre, I'm a classic
2. Some say I date back to ancient Egypt.
3. I'm very low-tech . . .
4. . . . but you can find me online.
5. I teach math concepts and help pass the time.
6. Matthew Broderick was a fan of mine in War Games.
7. The Brady Bunch borrows from me in its title sequence.
8. The Brits call me noughts and crosses.
9. To me, XO doesn't mean "kiss-hug."
10. Hollywood Squares is based on me.
    What am I?

1. I date back to the time of the ancient Egyptians.
2. In Jane Austen's day, men and women employed me.
3. My name can be used as a noun or a verb.
4. A new reality show on Lifetime is named after me.
5. Wine-lovers know me as an alternative to red or white.
6. I am thought to make you look more youthful.
7. I describe a pale shade of little girl's favorite color.
8. I'm used to emphasize cheekbones.
9. In French, I'm called rouge.
10. You can find me at the cosmetics counter.
    What am I?

1. I am 106 years old.
2. Many people visit me; most stay three nights.
3. I am home to a miniature Grand Canyon, and a tiger habitat.
4. Elvis is rumored to haunt me.
5. The Hoover Dam is my neighbor.
6. My name means "the meadows" in Spanish.
7. I'm the setting for a CSI series.
8. Nicolas Cage always wants to leave me.
9. I'm known as the "Wedding Capital of the World" . . .
10. . . . but I'm most famous for my casinos!
    Where am I?

1. In hot weather, I drink and drink and drink.
2. I trap pollution and help purify water.
3. I'm seedy, but I'm also beautiful.
4. Molasses is made from a type of me.
5. I'm green, but not with envy.
6. If I'm crabby, people get rid of me.
7. When in Kentucky, I'm blue.
8. At the White House, they have an Easter egg hunt on me.
9. I am the original tennis court surface.
10. Hula dancers think I make a great skirt.
    What am I?

1. I'm north of the equator.
2. I can see the Pacific Ocean.
3. I am part of a much larger city.
4. My fame began to grow in the Twentieth Century.
5. My products are exported around the globe.
6. There are lots of songs about me.
7. Judy Garland attended my high school.
8. My name can famously be seen on a hill.
9. My sidewalks have stars.
10. I am the movie capital of the world.
    Where am I?

1. I've been around for more than 100 years.
2. People of all ages adore me.
3. Elvis sang a song about me.
4. In Vermont, I have my own company.
5. My stuffing doesn't go with turkey.
6. I don't eat, but I'm usually very full.
7. Legend has it that a former U.S. president is my namesake.
8. I'm highly collectible.
9. Children like to give me hugs.
10. I'm related to Winnie and Paddington.
    What am I?

1. I am known for my smile.
2. I am male.
3. I wrote An Hour Before Daylight.
4. I use to be a farmer.
5. My middle name is Earl.
6. I like to build homes for other people.
7. I was the first U.S. president born in a hospital.
8. I lost my re-election bid to Ronald Reagan.
9. I won the Noble Peace Prize in 2002.
10. I was once governor of Georgia.
    Who am I?

1. I was an honorary Drug Enforcement agent.
2. I served in the U.S. Army.
3. My home is on the National Register of Historic Places.
4. I starred in 31 feature films and two documentaries.
5. I was inducted into the Rock and Roll Hall of Fame in 1986.
6. I gave my mom a pink Cadillac.
7. My ex-wife starred in TV's Dallas.
8. I was born in Tupelo, MS.
9. I'm known throughout the world by my first name.
10. I am "The King."
    Who am I?

1. I was born in 1945.
2. I trained as a ballet dancer.
3. My laugh is very recognizable.
4. I made my stage debut in Romeo and Juliet.
5. I made my film debut in The One and Only, Genuine, Original Family Band.
6. My autobiography A Lotus Grows in the Mud was published in 2005.
7. I've played an army private.
8. I won an Oscar for my role in Cactus Flower.
9. I have goldilocks, but I've never met the three bears.
10. Kurt Russell is my love.
    Who am I?

Page 1
I am the Grinch
I am Niagara Falls
I am Chocolate

Page 2
I am a Banana
I am Julia Roberts
I am a Bikini

Page 3
I am a Cranberry
I am Prince William
I am Tokyo

Page 4
I am Mount St. Helens
I am a Snowflake
I am Walt Disney World

Page 5
I am a Pumpkin
I am Paris
I am Dick Clark

Page 6
I am Rachael Ray
I am a Shopping Mall
I am Chopsticks

Page 7
I am a Lifeguard
I am a Rose
I am a Snowboard

Page 8
I am a Backpack
I am Stephenie Meyer
I am a Beanbag chair

Page 9
I am an iPod
I am Miami
I am a Doughnut

Page 10
I am a Diary
I am IKEA
I am Yoga

Page 11
I am a Snowman
I am Knitting
I am Dora the Explorer

Page 12
I am Tinker Bell
I am a Palm Tree
I am Fred Flintstone

Page 13
I am Montana
I am a Carpet
I am Sunglasses

Page 14
I am Gymnastics
I am Ugly Betty
I am Popcorn

Page 15
I am Luke Skywalker
I am a Stop sign
I am Olive oil

Page 16
I am a Jigsaw puzzle
I am Graceland
I am Frankenstein

Page 17
I am an Apple
I am a Grape
I am Julia Child

Page 18
I am Georgia O'Keeffe
I am Avon
I am Louisiana

Page 19
I am Texas
I am an Orange
I am Toothpaste

Page 20
I am New England
I am Mother Teresa
I am April

Page 21
I am a Taxi
I am Honolulu
I am Michael Flatley

Page 22
I am Milwaukee
I am Champagne
I am Jimmy Buffett

Page 23
I am a Roller Skate
I am a Picnic
I am Elizabeth Taylor

Page 24
I am Corn
I am John Lennon
I am American Idol

Page 25
I am John Grisham
I am the Circus
I am Alice in Wonderland

Page 26
I am a Sailboat
I am a Tie
I am a Pie

Page 27
I am Abraham Lincoln
I am a Hershey's kiss
I am a Teacher

Page 28
I am Jay Leno
I am a Hot Dog
I am Kenya

Page 29
I am Peter Pan
I am a Hamster
I am Washington D.C.

Page 30
I am a Hot-Air-Balloon
I am Yellowstone National Park
I am a Museum

Page 31
I am the Tooth Fairy
I am Up
I am Carrie Underwood

Page 32
I am Lemonade
I am Vancouver
I am Summer Camp

Page 33
I am Glee
I am Bill Gates
I am a Elf

Page 34
I am Google
I am a Fishing Pole
I am a Carrot

Page 35
I am a Monkey
I am Thunder
I am Kate Winslet

Page 36
I am a Grocery Store
I am a Airplane
I am Maple Syrup

Page 37
I am Francis Ford Coppola
I am Jerry Seinfeld
I am Gilligan

Page 38
I am Butter
I am a Radio Flyer Wagon
I am Dallas

Page 39
I am Winnie the Pooh
I am a Fire Engine
I am YouTube

Page 40
I am Honey
I am Amazon.com
I am Mr. Potato Head

Page 41
I am an iPhone
I am a Cactus
I am an Encyclopedia

Page 42
I am Where the Wild Things Are
I am Cinderella
I am a Kindle

Page 43
I am Eat, Pray, Love
I am Mamma Mia
I am Tea

Page 44
I am the Kentucky Derby
I am Gone With the Wind
I am Ellen DeGeneres

Page 45
I am Monopoly
I am Bread
I am an Election

Page 46
I am a Bowling ball
I am New Zealand
I am The Amazing Race

Page 47
I am Tiger Woods
I am the Grand Canyon
I am a Rainbow

Page 48
I am a Ostrich
I am a Contact lens
I am a Toothbrush

Page 49
I am Spam
I am Jamaica
I am Porky Pig

Page 50
I am Facebook
I am Pac-Man
I am a Compass

Page 51
I am a Crossword puzzle
I am a Baseball stadium
I am DNA

Page 52
I am Tic-tac-toe
I am Blush
I am Las Vegas

Page 53
I am Grass
I am Hollywood
I am a Teddy Bear

Page 54
I am Jimmy Carter
I am Elvis Presley
I am Goldie Hawn

www.ingramcontent.com/pod-product-compliance
Lightning Source LLC
Chambersburg PA
CBHW030524290526
45786CB00004B/1611